The Life and Times of
Saint Michael the Archangel
Wyatt North

Wyatt North Publishing

Foreword

One part biography, one part prayer book, **The Life and Prayers of Saint Michael the Archangel** is an essential book for any Christian.

Saint Michael is the Defender of the Faith and of our Church. As Christians we pray each day that he stands with us through this life and beyond.

Saint Michael the Archangel is the most revered archangel within the Church throughout history and today but his pre-eminence transcends the history of the Christian Church.

Saint Michael's role extends far beyond the war with the enemy here on Earth; it embraces every single member of the Church. His venerated name is invoked on a daily basis for protection, for healing, for consolation and by the dying as they make their final journey to God's Eternal Kingdom, seeking to avoid the desolation of Purgatory.

Enjoy.

Table of Contents

The Life of Saint Michael

At that time there shall arise Michael, the great prince, guardian of your people;
It shall be a time unsurpassed in distress since the nation began until that time.
At that time your people shall escape, everyone who is found written in the book' (Daniel 12:1)

.

Who Is Saint Michael?

V erses from Daniel prophesize the Day of Judgment; the day when Satan will finally be cast down into the abyss to face the curse of damnation for eternity. On this day, as it tells us in Scripture, the world will be free from mourning and loss. We do not know when that day will come, only God the Father knows the date and time of judgment.

In the meantime, faithful followers of Christ must tread their path carefully, following in the footsteps of Jesus Christ as they work out their salvation *'with fear and trembling.'* *(Philippians 2:12)*

Yet we are not alone as we walk that road less travelled. While we may sense the spiritual onslaught from all directions we need not fear. At our side, throughout our journey we have the prince who stands for the *'children of your people.'* (Daniel 12:1)

That prince is Saint Michael the Archangel, warrior of God, invincible and insurmountable. All angels of God's choir should be honoured, but Saint Michael above all of the angels and archangels stands revered through the ages. As the prophet Daniel makes clear, Saint Michael is indeed a prince among all of the angels.

Saint Michael is the Defender of the Faith and of our Church. As Christians we pray each day that he stands with us all and with our families through this life and beyond.

Saint Michael the Archangel is the most revered archangel within the Church throughout history and today but his pre-eminence transcends the history of the Christian Church.

His immortal name evolved from his outraged cry when the rebellious angel Lucifer dared to stand against God in the midst of the conflict of the heavenly hosts. In defending his God, Michael called out, 'MI-CHA-EL', 'Who is like unto God?' or 'Quis ut Deus' in Latin.

Who, after all, could ever compare to God?

And so it was - Saint Michael - a name which was to become synonymous through the centuries with a variety of roles but predominantly that of the Patron and Protector of the Church and the mighty Defender of the Faith.

Since his first defeat of Lucifer, at the command of his divine sovereign, Saint Michael has continued to protect the faithful on Earth, initially in his role of Guardian of the Israeli people in accordance with the Old Covenant. Later that same protection was provided to the Christian Church under the New Covenant.

Saint Michael's role extends far beyond the war with the enemy here on Earth; it embraces every single member of the Church. His venerated name is invoked on a daily basis for protection, for healing, for consolation and by the dying as they make their final journey to God's Eternal Kingdom, seeking to avoid the desolation of Purgatory.

Saint Michael the Archangel is the head of God's heavenly throng, offering divine fortitude and protecting the souls of the faithful as they fight against the powers of evil seeking to overturn the throne of Almighty God and rule the world. God's angels willingly submit to his command. After God, it is Saint Michael to whom they owe their eternal peace and joy, the archangel who seeks only to God's will. .

It was Saint Michael who was at God's side before the beginning of time, playing a pivotal role in the first defeat of Lucifer, as he will on the final Day of Judgment.

It is Saint Michael who provides consolation to departed souls lingering in purgatory who seek only to reach the Paradise of God's Eternal Kingdom.

It is Saint Michael who walks with those souls as they depart their mortal bodies to face judgment for their mortal lives.

It is Saint Michael who valiantly protects both the Church and the Blessed Sacrament.

It is Saint Michael who is pre-eminent among the holiest of heavenly hosts, the angels and archangels.

Ultimately, it is Saint Michael who will lead God's angels, blessed with the power of light and grace, to victory over Satan and his fallen angels in the final battle. We see this prophesied in the verse from Daniel and depicted in the Book of Revelation.

It is Saint Michael who will sound the last trumpet and throw Satan and his allies into the burning depths of eternal damnation.

Saint Michael has been and remains protector and friend to Christians around the world, both today and through the centuries. We can rely on him and trust him. We know that a life lived invoking him to be our intercessor and our guardian angel will bring us the ultimate promise of eternal life when the Day of Judgment arrives.

He is the only archangel referred to by name in Scripture, a figure of reverence throughout the history of Christian art.

St Francis de Sales once claimed "Veneration of Saint Michael is the great remedy against despising the rights of God, against insubordination, skepticism and infidelity." Today, in the often-moral-abyss of the 21st Century it seems our need for him is greater than ever in countless daily conflicts of spiritual warfare.

Through it all Saint Michael is with us. He will take our hand through our 'fear and trembling'. He will heed and respond to our heartfelt prayers.

Saint Michael: Prince of Heavenly Hosts, Protector of the Church, Advocate of the Dying, Consoler of Souls, Guardian of the Blessed Sacrament and His Holiness the Pope.

Saint Michael: The archangel without equal.

Angels and Archangels

The beauty, transcendence, wisdom and holiness of the angels flows into Christian lives by the grace of God. Angels are intelligent spiritual beings, who, like men and women, have their own free will. Being capable of sin, they too could choose whether to worship or turn away from God.

In understanding Saint Michael's role within God's realms and within Christian lives it is useful to understand the dominions of angels and their roles within the Bible and place within God's eternal kingdom.

Within Holy Scripture, we find nine separate groups of angels:

Seraphim. The seraphim appear most prominently in Isaiah, *'Seraphim were stationed above; each of them had six wings: with two they covered their faces, with two they covered their feet, and with two they hovered. One cried out to the other: 'Holy, holy, holy is the Lord of hosts! All the earth is filled with his glory!' (Isaiah 6:2)*

Cherubim

Thrones

Dominions

Powers

Virtues

Principalities

Archangels

Angels

We also find references to four angel choirs in Colossians:

'For in him were created all things in heaven and on earth, the visible and the invisible, whether thrones or dominions or principalities or powers;
all things were created through him and for him.' (Colossians 1:16)

These groups of angel choirs are the only groups that have been revealed to us through God's Word. The highest choir is that of the Seraphim while the choir of Angels is the lowest. It is the Angels, who are closest to humans and our material world.

Angels in the Bible are deemed to be beings of light, blessed with supernatural grace by God. They cannot perform miracles in their own strength but only as God wills them to do so. Appointed to protect the human race as His messengers, their principal role is of knowing and loving God and protecting His throne.

A familiar image of a biblical angel that comes to mind is that of the appearance of the Angel Gabriel to the Blessed Virgin Mary foretelling of the birth of Jesus Christ in Luke's gospel. Further references to angels are apparent throughout the Bible and particularly in the Psalms.

In Psalm 91, the role of angels within God's kingdom is made very clear:

'For he commands his angels with regard to you, to guard you wherever you go.' (Psalm 91:11)

Archangels

An archangel is a supernatural being taking a unique place among God's angels. The word archangel is derived from the Green 'archaggelos' and only two specific references to archangels in the Bible are to be found.

The first is in 1 Thessalonians, the second we find in Jude.

'For the Lord himself, with a word of command, with the voice of an archangel and with the trumpet of God, will come down from heaven, and the dead in Christ will rise first.' (1 Thess 4:16)

'Yet the archangel Michael, when he argued with the devil in a dispute over the body of Moses, did not venture to pronounce a reviling judgment* upon him but said, "May the Lord rebuke you!" (Jude 9)

Saint Michael is deemed supreme among all of the angels, bestowed with command over all of the heavenly hosts. As we can see in the verse from Jude, he is the only archangel referred to by name. This is not to diminish the other angels; it simply reflects Saint Michael's elevated status before God within their ranks.

Holy Scripture names only three angels. Jewish tradition on the other hand gives us seven archangels. All seven of these archangels appear in the apocryphal Book of Enoch, which we will look at in the next section. In this latter book, four angels take the most prominent roles, lead by Saint Michael.

The angels named in Scripture are Saint Michael, St Raphael and St Gabriel.

St Gabriel: Known as 'Strength of God' he is renowned throughout Christian history for appearing to the Virgin Mary to announce the coming of Jesus Christ.

St Raphael: Raphael's name is interpreted as 'Healing of God'. We see him in the Book of Tobit when he cures Tobit's eyes with a tender healing touch.

Saint Michael: *'Who is like unto God?'* Saint Michael is the archangel called to perform mighty deeds in the name of God to demonstrate His omnipotence. No one is equal to God and his awesome might and power is glorified through Saint Michael. This ultimate power is emphasized in the final book of the New Testament, which epitomizes Saint Michael's role among the Christian Church. His power and supremacy is a gift from God.

Saint Michael surpasses all of the other archangels in glory described by both St Peter and St Jude Thaddeus as an angel of superior rank.

Lucifer and the Fallen Angels

The angels were originally created as spirits of light and love surrounding God's heavenly throne. On one momentous occasion God decided to test the loyalty of His angels. This test was the revelation by God of the future incarnation of His son. As he presented a vision of the birth of Jesus Chris, He simultaneously revealed the glory of the Virgin Mary as the Blessed Mother of Jesus, who was also to be revered by all of the angels.

At that time, the angel Lucifer reveled in his status as an exalted prince in heaven. He was gifted beyond measure yet nursed latent ambitions, which were to be his downfall. When Lucifer learned that a mere mortal was to be the mother of God's son – a human who he would have to bow down to – his anger knew no bounds.

In his rage, he rebelled against God, yelling *'I will be like the most High!'* (Isaiah 14:14) From Lucifer's rage and unstoppable ambition emerged the beginning of original sin and the first sinful thought.

'How you have fallen from the heavens, O morning star, son of the dawn! Have you have been down to the earth, you who conquered nations! In your heart you said 'I will scale the heavens' Above the stars of God I will set up my throne; I will take my seat on the Mount of Assembly on the heights of Zaphon. I will ascend above the tops of the clouds, I will be like the Most High!' No! Down to Sheol you will be brought to the depths of the pit!' (Isaiah 14:12-15)

According to Isaiah, Lucifer's downfall was the result of the twin sins of pride and ambition.

In the battle at the end of time, which parallels that at the beginning, Revelation tells us how Lucifer's offended pride and malicious ambition swept through the angels like a plague, affecting almost one third of the heavenly choirs. .

'Its tail swept away a third of the stars in the sky and hurled them down to the earth.' (Rev 12:4)

Yet as we have seen and will see again, one angel stood against them with his rally cry 'Who is like unto God?' That angel was Saint Michael.

'Then war broke out in heaven; Michael and his angels battled against the dragon. The dragon and its angels fought back, but they did not prevail and there was no longer any place for them in heaven. The huge dragon, the ancient serpent, who is called the Devil and Satan, who deceived the whole world, was thrown down to earth, and its angels were down with it.' (Revelation 12:7-9)

As it will be in the end, so it was in the beginning. Saint Michael with his legions of angels will emerge victorious over Lucifer and his allies.

It is here that the apocryphal Book of Enoch enhances our understanding of the crucial role played by our Protector and Warrior after Lucifer and his band of sinful angels fell to Earth.

Saint Michael and the Book of Enoch

The Book of Enoch is one of several apocryphal books which stands outside of Scripture yet explains several enigmatic references within Genesis. An apocryphal book refers to Biblical or related writings not forming part of the accepted canon of Scripture.

Saint Michael is only specifically referred to on a handful of occasions in the Bible. The Book of Enoch enables us to learn more about his pre-eminence among the angels.

For centuries the Church accepted The Book of Enoch until its final rejection as Scripture at the Council of Laodicea in 364. Its contents nevertheless shed light upon our understanding of both the Old and New Testaments with glimpses of the Apocalypse, brief sightings of Noah, and its theme of triumph of good over evil.

Today, it is actively used mainly by the Ethiopian Church yet is still considered to be one of the most important apocryphal books outside of the Bible. Without doubt it illuminates our understanding of Saint Michael when we come to Revelation in the New Testament and is awash with the concepts of original sin, fallen angels, demonology and the Day of Judgment.

Enoch is mentioned only briefly in the Bible in Genesis 5:24 when he disappears without explanation:

'Enoch walked with God and then he was no longer here, for God took him.'

He does not feature as a major presence in either the Old Testament or the New Testament but he is praised as a man of great faith in Hebrews:

'By faith Enoch was taken up so that he should not see death, and he was found no more because God had taken him. Before he was taken up, he was attested to have pleased God.' (Hebrews 11:5)

If we read further on in Genesis we find a reference to *'sons of God' (Gen 6:2)* taking mortal women as wives. These 'sons of God' referred to in Genesis are collectively called 'The Watchers' in the Book of Enoch; the fallen angels defeated by Saint Michael at the beginning of time.

Tradition tells of the Watchers descending to earth and defiling human women, leading to the origin of evil and the magnification of sin in the world. The children of these sinful unions are malevolent giants walking the earth, seeking only to cause havoc and destroy.

We first encounter Saint Michael in the company of three other archangels, Sariel, Raphael and Gabriel. Distressed by the events on earth and the misery inflicted on mankind by the giants, they implore God to act. God's response is to present each archangel with a mission. Raphael is tasked to bind fallen angel Asael and heal the earth of the wounds inflicted by the Watchers.

Gabriel is sent to destroy the gigantic offspring of these forbidden unions.

Saint Michael is dispatched to Shemihazah and his companions to:

'bind them for seventy generations in valleys of the earth until the Great Day of their condemnation.' (Chapter 10:12, the Book of Enoch)

Afterwards they will be cast into the fire to burn for eternity.

These events form the basis of God's ultimate judgment on the Earth, bringing about the floods that destroy mankind. It is Enoch's grandson Noah and his family who will emerge as sole survivors of this destruction, warned by an unnamed angel (possibly believed to be Saint Michael) as they are instructed to build the Ark.

The presence of the archangels plays a vital role in the early parts of The Book of Enoch with many visions of Michael, Raphael, Gabriel and Phanuel throughout. Enoch also describes how these same four archangels are responsible for escorting God whenever He leaves his throne.

Saint Michael's pre-eminence in God's kingdom is also apparent as he is given the role of overseeing human virtue in order to guide the nations. Saint Michael is described as:

'one of the holy angels – set over the best part of mankind and over chaos.'
(Enoch 20:5)

and later presented as 'the first' angel:

'The first is Michael, the merciful and long-suffering' (Enoch 40:9)

Saint Michael is also heard to *'bless the Lord of the Spirits forever and ever.' (Enoch 40:4)*

It is also Saint Michael who commands an angel to raise Enoch up in his distress over God's punishment of the Watchers (*Enoch 60*). In a spectacularly vivid presentation of heaven, Saint Michael again takes Enoch's hand to show him all the *'secrets of the ends of the heavens.' (Enoch 71)* Enoch is subsequently taken to a house above the heavens circled by a myriad of angels protecting the throne of God.

Throughout the Book of Enoch, it is Saint Michael who is always first among the angels, Saint Michael who sends an angel to raise Enoch's spirit, and Saint Michael who leads him above heaven to discover the carefully guarded secrets of the cosmos.

Further References to Saint Michael

Saint Michael is mentioned in other Biblical and associated writings, always as a powerful figure, prince of the angels.

Traditional Jewish Writings and Saint Michael

Rabbinic Jewish writings reveal Michael acting as Israel's advocate and occasionally battling with the princes of other nations, specifically the fallen angel Samael, who is Israel's accuser. His role as protector and warrior is again echoed here.

Saint Michael in the Dead Sea Scrolls

The Dead Sea Scrolls discovered between 1947 and 1956 clearly show Saint Michael as an angelic savior figure. In one particular scroll – The War Scroll – the story of a forty-year war is recounted. This battle is fought between the Sons of Light and the Sons of Darkness. The Sons of Light are led by Saint Michael who yet again emerges victorious over the forces of darkness as the prophet Daniel always predicted it.

Revelation of Moses

In a further apocryphal book, 'Revelation of Moses' Saint Michael guards the body of Eve.

Saint Michael in the Bible

*T*hen war broke out in heaven; Michael and his angels battled
against the dragon. The dragon and its angels fought back, but they
did not prevail and there was no longer any place for them in
heaven. The huge dragon, the ancient serpent, who is called the
Devil and Satan, who deceived the whole world, was thrown down to
earth, and its angels were thrown down with it. (Revelation 12:7-9)

For many Christians these words epitomize Saint Michael's
character and God's ultimate purpose for him. They are the
most famous words relating to Saint Michael throughout
Scripture.

While specific references to Saint Michael occur only on a few
occasions, the Church believes that the many reference to
angels of God at vital times in Biblical history are the presence
of Saint Michael.

According to Christian tradition it was Saint Michael who first
led Adam into the Garden of Eden at the beginning of time. It
was Saint Michael again who, after the Fall, stood at the gates
of Paradise waiting for Adam:-

'He expelled the man, stationing the cherubim and the fiery
revolving sword east of the Garden of Eden, to guard the way to the
tree of life.' (Genesis 3:24)

Saint Michael is also believed to have been the angel who
informed Abraham that God would make him father of all of
the people.

As God revealed himself to Moses at the burning bush, it is believed that Saint Michael was the angel of the Lord who appeared to him (Exodus 3:2). Similarly, it is thought that Saint Michael was the angel selected to glorify God at the miraculous parting of the waters as the Israeli people fled their Egyptian pursuers to escape from slavery. Yet again, it was Saint Michael who presented the Ten Commandments to Moses at Mount Sinai.

In Numbers, the identity of the 'Angel of the Lord' sent to Balaam is also considered to be Saint Michael *(Numbers 22:22)*. Finally, in 2 Kings, we see Saint Michael the Warrior destroying the army of Sennacherib at their Assyrian camp.

That night the angel of the Lord went forth and struck down one hundred and eighty-five thousand men in the Assyrian camp. Early the next morning, there they were, dead, all those corpses!' (2 Kings 19:35)

Yet there is more to be revealed as suggested in Jude when he makes the one and only reference to an archangel – namely Saint Michael – in Scripture:

'Yet the archangel Michael, when he argued with the devil in a dispute over the body of Moses did not venture to pronounce a reviling judgment upon him but say 'May the Lord rebuke you!' (Jude 1:9)

Here Jude refers to a story from the apocryphal 'Assumption of Moses.' While the Bible briefly mentions that Moses was buried, Jude's fleeting comment concerns Saint Michael given the task of burying Moses. As he arrived, he was challenged by Satan. Deftly, Saint Michael concealed Moses' tomb from both Satan and the Israelites. The latter was to prevent worship of false idols. It also shows that, despite being provoked, Saint Michael does not revile Satan.

In addition to Revelation and Jude, Saint Michael's name is recorded in Daniel:

'…but the Prince of the Kingdom of Persia stood in my way for 21 days until finally Michael, one of the chief princes, came to help me. I left him there with the Prince of Persia' (Daniel 10:12).

He is also referred to as *'Michael, your Prince'* in Daniel 10:21

Finally, as we have seen, Daniel predicts Saint Michael's triumphant role at the end of time:

'At that time there shall arise Michael, the great prince, guardian of your people;
It shall be a time unsurpassed in distress since the nation began until that time.
At that time your people shall escape, everyone who is found written in the book.' (Daniel 12:1)

It is interesting to note that all of the three Old Testament references to Michael refer to him by using the word prince or princes. As protector of the Church and Defender of the Faith, of guardian of Christian souls, he above all of the angels is surely worthy of that accolade.

The Offices of Saint Michael

To grow spiritually, all Christians need to invoke Saint Michael as guardian of their souls and bodies on a daily basis. He can protect us through temptations, protect us from danger and gain God's grace through his intercession. He imbues us with virtue, he is obedient to our Savior Jesus Christ and stands near to Mary, the Mother of God.

He is a friend to all Christians, who can pray to Saint Michael for help in the midst of personal struggles and on behalf of the Christian Church during embattled times of spiritual warfare.

As prince among the angels he has several offices within the Church.

Advocate of the Dying

Daily devotion to Saint Michael in this life will ensure he is waiting to receive your soul at the hour of your death and lead you to the Eternal Kingdom. The souls of all of the faithful are delivered by God to Saint Michael for him to bring to God on the Day of Judgment. As we die our souls are open to last minute attacks by Satan's demons yet by invoking Saint Michael protection is ensured through his shield. On reaching the judgment seat of Christ, Saint Michael will intercede on our behalf and beg for our forgiveness. The Church immortalizes the name of Saint Michael in its prayers for the dead.

'May the holy standard-bearer, Michael, introduce them into that holy light which Thou didst promise of old to Abraham and his descendants.'

Consoler of Poor Souls

Saint Michael is also called upon in this vital role to protect souls against not only the malevolent spirits who would seek to possess them but of the humans who would do them harm during their lives on earth. This is not some arbitrary decision, it is vital to all believers to deal with the reality of the world. Trust your family and friends to him and invoke his support every day for all of those you love, praying especially for his defense at the end of your life. Christians can also invoke Saint Michael for those who have already departed to be taken to Heaven and not to be left in the darkness of Purgatory. If we truly desire to be led into the Eternal Kingdom to reside in the presence of God, we must invoke Saint Michael's guidance and protection throughout our lives.

Guardian of the Blessed Sacrament and the Pope

Saint Michael guards the Blessed Sacrament and altars throughout the world. During the service of a Solemn High Mass it is Michael to whom the priest turns to for intercession. He also speaks these words during the Offertory Mass of Saint Michael:

'An angel stood near the altar of the Temple, having a golden censer in his hand, and there was given to him much incense; and the smoke of the perfumes ascended before God.'

Saint Michael has protected God's people throughout history. He protected the Ark of the Covenant and the Tabernacle. Today he protects the Eucharist, accompanying it wherever it goes. It is Saint Michael's name that is invoked throughout Holy Mass and is presented as the bearer of incense and the intercessor before God's throne.

Saint Michael's devotion to the Holy Eucharist of our Lord Jesus Christ and His Holiness the Pope is boundless.

Prince of the Heavenly Hosts

Saint Michael stands supreme above all of the Archangels. The Church agrees with the Greek Fathers in placing Saint Michael above all of the other angels, giving him the highest ranking of 'Archistrategos' - 'highest general'. Being first to announce the Savior to the angel choirs when God revealed his will, Saint Michael also enjoys unprecedented status as the 'first Christian' and the 'first Apostle of Christ'.

He is also first lieutenant of Jesus Christ as it is he who will lead God's armies to victory against the enemy when the Day of Judgment arrives.

No-one knows when this day and hour of judgment will come. Jesus forecasts signs of war and famine:

You will hear of wars and reports of wars; see that you are not alarmed, for these things must happen, but it will not yet be the end. Nation will rise against nation and kingdom against kingdom; there will be famines and earthquakes form place to place... and then many will be led into sin' they will betray and hate one another.' (Matthew 24:6-7 &10)

Such words are as relevant today as they have been through the ages. Yet again Saint Michael will play a vital role in waging battle against Satan as revealed in Daniel's prophecy in 12:1. As the final trumpet sounds when Satan is cast into the abyss it is Saint Michael who will be our advocate.

Protector of the Church

As we have seen, Saint Michael has defended and protected Christians throughout Old Testament times and protects Christ's Church today. Today, we live in what seems to be an inward-looking, self-centered world. The path of the Church as a beacon of light in this world is strewn with humanity's discarded morals. To grow in our faith and for the protection of the Church and all Christians around the world we are in need of Saint Michael more than ever.

Helper and Defender of All Christians

In his role as Protector of the Church, Saint Michael is our advocate; the protector and defender of every single Christian and of all Christian nations throughout the world. Whoever confesses the faith and follows in the footsteps of Jesus Christ engenders the protection of this glorious archangel Saint Michael, to defend us from temptations and the daily onslaught of spiritual warfare.

Healer of the Sick

Apparitions of Saint Michael throughout the ages have often coincided with times of great healing, especially in the early ages of the Church. Our next chapter looks at some of these apparitions, including miracles of healing performed by our heavenly physician, the healer who we are encouraged to invoke in so many areas of our lives as we live out our Christian faith.

Veneration of Saint Michael

Saint Michael is revered in Church liturgy for defending Christians against Satan from the beginning of time.

In the early days of the Church, the following prayer was offered:

'*Lord, Jesus Christ, King of Glory, deliver the souls of all the faithful departed from the pains of Hell and from the deep pit; deliver them from the mouth of the lion that Hell may not swallow them up and that they may not fall into darkness, but may the standard-bearer Michael conduct them into the holy light, which thou didst promise of old to Abraham and his seed. We offer to thee, Lord, sacrifices and prayers; do thou receive them in behalf of those souls whom we commemorate this day. Grant them, Lord, to pass from death to that life which thou didst promise of old to Abraham and to his seed.*'

In the 13th century Saint Michael was invoked together with the Blessed Virgin Mary, Saint John, Saint Peter, and Saint Paul:

'*Saint Michael the Archangel, defend us in battle! Be our protection against the wickedness and snares of the devil. May God rebuke him, we humbly pray, and do thou, O Prince of the heavenly host, by the power of God, thrust into Hell Satan and all the other evil spirits who roam about the world seeking the ruin of souls.*'

Saint Michael also features heavily in the Rite of Exorcism, where the priest will pray:

'Most glorious Prince of the Heavenly Army, Holy Michael the Archangel, defend us in battle against the princes and powers and rulers of darkness in this world, against the spiritual iniquities of those former angels. Come to the help of man whom God made in his own image and whom he bought from the tyranny of Satan at a great price. The Church venerates you as her custodian and patron. The Lord confided to your care all the souls of those redeemed, so that you would lead them to happiness in Heaven. Pray to the God of peace that he crush Satan under our feet; so that Satan no longer be able to hold men captive and thus injure the Church. Offer our prayers to the Most High God, so that His mercies be given us soon. Make captive that Animal, that Ancient serpent, which is enemy and Evil Spirit, and reduce it to everlasting nothingness, so that it no longer seduce the nations.'

He is also especially celebrated on Saint Michaelmas Day (Feast of Saint Michael) on September 29th each year.

Honoring the Angels (Saint Michaelmas Day)

As God's holy messengers sent to comfort and strengthen His people, the angels as a whole are worthy of veneration. In the words of Pope John Paul II:

'...the Church confesses her faith in the guardian angels, venerating them in the liturgy with an appropriate feast and recommending recourse to their protection by frequent prayer.'

History of the Feast of the Archangels Michael, Raphael, and Gabriel

Feast days for saints emanated from early Christian traditions that remembered Christian martyrs on the anniversaries of their deaths. Rejoicing for their new lives in heaven has always been an integral part of the celebrations.

In medieval times, the Feast of Saint Michael was also known as Michaelmas Day. On that day Christians were required to invoke special prayers to the heavenly archangel.

In medieval England, Michaelmas represented the time to pay quarterly bills for the third quarter of the year. Irish Catholics also celebrated with banquets in honor of Saint Michael, eating copious amounts of blackberries. Legend has it that the blackberries fell onto Satan when he was defeated by Saint Michael, thus creating a bitter taste.

Following extensive theological reform in the 18th century Michaelmas Day was no longer an obligatory feast, but Christians around the world were encouraged to continue the celebrations in honor of Saint Michael.

In 1921, the feast formally became the Feast of Saint Michael, Saint Gabriel, and Saint Raphael by order of the Vatican. Anglican sections of the Church combine this feast with a celebration for all of the guardian angels on 2nd October each year.

Feast of the Apparition of Saint Michael – May 8th

The Feast of the Apparition of Saint Michael was celebrated until 1969 on May 8th every year following the archangel's appearance at Monte Gargano.

Celebrations Today

The unstinting devotion to Saint Michael unifies the Church across East and West as both invoke his assistance. His apparition at Mont Saint Michel was also celebrated on October 16th and other parts of the church continue their own individual celebrations.

Today, Catholics are encouraged to attend mass, read Scripture or pray in thankfulness for the protection afforded by the angels to both themselves and the Church. All of the angels offer God's protection to Christians, without exception.

You may wish to use the following devotion on the angels' Feast Day. Take some time to settle comfortably in a quiet space alone. Be ready to accept God's presence and immerse yourself in his love as you wait for Saint Michael's words.

Read Revelation Chapter 12:7-12 especially focusing on how Saint Michael and his angels defeat Satan.

Notice Saint Michael's rapid response to evil, it is swift and decisive.

Picture the scene. See how quickly God sends Saint Michael to destroy the darkness.

Focus on an area of personal fear, despair or hopelessness in your own life where you feel the need for divine intervention.

Visualize the area as a dark form, poised to attack.

Ask for God's permission to attack that fear or distress, whatever type of personal darkness it may be.

Now visualize Saint Michael according to the description in Revelation, defeating that fear just as he defeated Satan.

Spend several minutes resplendent in light as Saint Michael triumphs over the symbolic demons of fear and despair in God's name.

Give thanks to God for this healing. As you thank Him, read the end refer, referring back to the end of the Revelation passage, where John rejoices in Satan's fall.

Saint Michael was God's first angel. As prince among all of the angels and archangels he gives us courage, strength and integrity, protecting the Church and all Christians with his flaming sword.

Visions of Saint Michael Through the Ages

Visions of Saint Michael have been recorded throughout the centuries from the springs at Colossae to calling St Joan of Arc to fulfill God's purpose for her life.

Colossae

The spring at Colossae is said to have been drawn from the rock by Saint Michael. As pagans attempted to destroy the sanctuary of Saint Michael, the archangel himself shot a lightning bolt at the rock to split it, forever sanctifying the waters that flow from within.

Constantine the Great

Saint Michael appeared to Constantine in the fourth century, helping him to achieve victory in battle against Emperor Maxentius. When Constantine erected a church in honor of Saint Michael, he appeared to Constantine in person, declaring:

'I am Michael, the chief of the angelic legions of the Lord of hosts, the protector of the Christian religion, who while you were battling against godless tyrants, placed the weapons in your hands.'

Known as the 'Michaelion' the sick used to sleep in the church invoking his name and waiting patiently for his healing. This revered location was the scene of numerous miracles over the following centuries.

Monte Gargano

During the Middle Ages, devotion to Saint Michael grew in strength and he appeared in many apparitions. Before the 9th century, Saint Michael was the only Archangel to whom liturgical feasts were held in his honor. This was nothing to do with the apparitions and everything to do with his strength, his power in intercession and his protection of the Church. It is his appearance at Monte Gargano which resulted in the Feast of the Apparition of Saint Michael which was formally celebrated on 8th May each year until the late 1960s.

Its history dates back to 404 in Monte Gargano in Italy on the land of a wealthy man. On herding his cattle at the end of a day he found he was missing a steer which he eventually discovered on a mountain peak. The animal refused to leave and his owner shot an arrow towards it in frustration. The arrow ricocheted and wounded the wealthy man who sought the wise counsel of the Bishop of Siponto.

 As the Bishop prayed to God to reveal His will Saint Michael appeared declaring:

'I am Michael, the Archangel, who ever stand before the Lord. I am keeping this place under my special protection. By this strange occurrence, I wish to remind men to celebrate the Divine service in my honor and that of all the Angels.'

Immediately afterwards, the Bishop, accompanied by the townspeople, went to the mountain invoking Saint Michael to intercede before God for them. On arrival they discovered an entrance and stairway. From that time onwards, devoted pilgrims flocked to that place to worship God and pray for Saint Michael to intercede.

That is not the sole apparition of Saint Michael recorded at Monte Gargano. Around the late 13th century St Oringa noted a 'beautiful youth' leading vulnerable maidens on a pilgrimage to safety from a band of robbers posing as guides. The 'beautiful youth' is believed to have been Saint Michael.

Joan of Arc

St Joan famously attributed her victories against the English in the 15th century to Saint Michael who appeared to her in visions. Her first encounter with the archangel occurred as she tended her flock of sheep at the age of 13. It was Saint Michael, along with Saints Catherine and Margaret, who were to be her guides throughout her short life.

Gregory the Great

During the time of Saint Gregory the Great in the 6th century a terrible plague hit the city of Rome. As the Pope prayed he carried a statue of the Blessed Virgin Mary. At the castle of Saint Angelo, Saint Michael appeared holding a sword. As he returned it to its scabbard, the plague miraculously vanished.

Egyptian Christians

Egyptian Christians placed their iconic River Nile under Saint Michael's protection, commemorating him on the 12th day of each month. Today they maintain June 2nd as the feast of Michael for the rising of the Nile.

The Vision of Pope Leo XIII

On October 13, 1884, Pope Leo XIII completed mass along with his cardinals and without warning collapsed into a deep spiritual ecstasy. In those brief moments he experienced a terrifying vision of a confrontation between Jesus and Satan. During this confrontation, he saw countless evil demons released from the depths of hell to fight against the church. Yet in the midst of this apocalyptic scene appeared Saint Michael, in his role as valiant warrior, casting the demons back into the depths of the pit once more.

For His Holiness Pope Leo, this was sufficient and incontrovertible proof of Saint Michael's conquering powers. As a result, he wrote the Leonine Exorcism which he ordered to be repeated at the end of every service of mass in every Christian Church throughout the world.

This honorary prayer remained in regular use until 1934 when it was replaced by an abbreviated prayer.

The Original Prayer to Saint Michael

The original prayer written by Pope Leon was nearly six hundred words long, the words below are an abridged version:

'O Glorious Archangel St. Michael, Prince of the heavenly host, be our defense in the terrible warfare which we carry on against principalities and Powers, against the rulers of this world of darkness, spirits of evil. Come to the aid of man, whom God created immortal, made in his own image and likeness, and redeemed at a great price from the tyranny of the devil. Fight this day the battle of the Lord, together with the holy angels, as already thou hast fought the leader of the proud angels, Lucifer, and his apostate host, who were powerless to resist thee, nor was there place for them any longer in Heaven....'

The New Prayer to Saint Michael

The revised prayer was much shorter at only fifty nine words long:

'Saint Michael the Archangel, defend us in battle, be our protection against the wickedness and snares of the devil; may God rebuke him, we humbly pray; and do thou, O Prince of the heavenly host, by the power of God, thrust into hell Satan and all evil spirits who wander through the world for the ruin of souls. Amen.'

Today this particular prayer in honor of Saint Michael is no longer recited at mass, although the reasons for the decision to cease the recital are not documented.

The complete versions of both prayers are available in the Prayers to Saint Michael section of this book.

Representations of Saint Michael in Christian Art

e image of Saint Michael the Archangel is ubiquitous throughout the history of Christian art. We find him in paintings, stained glass windows, manuscripts, architecture and endless other depictions. It is impossible to describe or include the endless portrayals of our Defender of the Faith in such a confined space yet will we attempt to give a flavor of his heavenly inspiration to early Christian artists.

Saint Michael as Warrior

The common portrayal of Saint Michael is often as a winged warrior clad in battle armor and wielding a sword or spear. The art used for this book's cover, for example, provides the iconic image of Saint Michael.

Often he will tower triumphantly over an image of Satan sporting emblems of a banner, a sword, a dragon and scales. The scales represent the scales of justice to weigh the souls of the departed and the book is the book of life against which departing souls will be judged. His shield often bears the Latin inscription *'Quis ut Deus': 'Who is like unto God.'*

Saint Michael the Weigher of Souls

Before the Renaissance period, beginning in Italy during the 14th century, portrayals of Saint Michael saw him represented in a more peaceful role than that of warrior. In the early history of the Christian church Saint Michael carried only the scales of justice. Post-Renaissance, the verses from Revelation gripped the imagination of the artists of the time until they evolved into the universal images of warrior and protector that we see today.

Scripture does not show us Saint Michael as Weigher of Souls. This image is derived from his heavenly offices of Advocate of the Dying and Consoler of Souls, believed to have begun in Egyptian and Greek art. We know it is Saint Michael who accompanies the faithful in their final hour and to their own day of judgment, interceding on our behalf before Christ. In doing so he balances the good deeds of our lives against the bad, epitomized by the scales.

It is in this context also that his image can be found on dooms paintings (representing the Day of Judgment), on countless church walls, and carved over church doorways. Pre-Renaissance, Saint Michael was often shown wearing sumptuous garments, carrying a scepter in place of his spear. The words *'Holy Holy Holy'* inscribed within these depictions suggest Byzantine influences. On occasion, Saint Michael is presented alongside Gabriel, with both of them wearing purple and white tunics.

Changing Images of Saint Michael

The subtle shift from peaceful purveyor of souls to archangel of destruction emanates from German culture. When the Germanic tribes of the Lombards invaded Italy in the 6th century they brought with them a culture inspired by Wotan, a dragon slaying God. Some suggest it is this influence which played a role in the changing artistic representations of Saint Michael.

In addition, the Monte Gargano shrine of Saint Michael lay in Lombard territory. Here, one of the earliest portrayals of Saint Michael's victory over Satan was presented in bronze. This depiction also intriguingly finds Satan portrayed in human form. It is possible that this, coupled with the warlike traditions of the Lombards influenced the shift in Saint Michael's image in art.

The most famous portrayal of Saint Michael in his victorious role is found in Michelangelo's painting of the Sistine Chapel in the Vatican in Rome.

Saint Michael in 'Paradise Lost'

In the famous classic English poet John Milton, Saint Michael is shown advising Adam that if he strives to learn about the limitations of man's knowledge and embraces 'charity' then he will enjoy *'A paradise within thee, happier far.'*

For Milton, Saint Michael personifies the transforming joy of inner peace. In Milton's eyes, man is much happier with inner peace outside of the Garden of Eden than he is remaining there without it.

The poet's words also echo how vital it is to remain strong in personal faith, even in the face persecution or condemnation. In support of this suggestion, Saint Michael shows Adam a vision of Enoch and Noah, who both risked their own lives to follow God's calling, such was the strength of the faith.

Written in the 17th Century after Milton had lost his sight, this epic poem also tells of Saint Michael's triumph over evil in Revelation:

'They dreaded worse than Hell; so much the fear
Of thunder and the sword of Michael
Wrought still within them.'

Additional Representations in Art

One of the finest ivory carvings in existence today can be found on an ivory diptych (a pair of writing tablets carved on the outside) in the British Museum in London, England. Within the carving, Saint Michael is represented as a stately figure holding the orb of sovereignty in his right hand. In the left hand is his scepter – typical of early artistic depictions of the archangel. It is likely that it originated from Constantinople around the 4th Century.

The British museum is also home to a miniature of Saint Michael from around 1400 with a portrayal of the Apocalypse and the following inscription in Latin:

'Then war broke out in heaven; Michael* and his angels battled against the dragon. The dragon and its angels fought back but they did not prevail and there was no longer any place for them in heaven.' (Revelation 12:7-8)

Visitors to Bourges Cathedral in France will find a sculpture of Saint Michael over the central door of the cathedral dating back to the thirteenth century. Here his scales are weighted in favor of the vulnerable soul whose fate he is called to intervene on.

It is impossible to offer more than a flavor of the prominence of Saint Michael in Christian art. From Raphael's classic paintings on display in the iconic Louvre museum in Paris to icons found in the remote St Catherine's Monastery on Mount Sinai, he has inspired the imagination of Christians throughout the ages. The legacy of the early Christian period in particular continues to be a source of reassurance to all Christians today.

.

Prayers to Saint Michael

The Church encourages all Christians to develop a regular devotion to Saint Michael through prayer and in the way we live our daily lives. Saint Michael glorifies God not only through his own actions, but also in helping others to understand and fulfill God's purpose for their lives.

God's holy angels provide divine protection but we must invoke them to enjoy their blessings. These prayers may assist in those daily devotions.

The Angelic Crown or Chaplet

(Chaplet of Saint Michael the Archangel)

In 1751, Saint Michael the Archangel appeared to a Portuguese Carmelite nun, Antonia d'Astonac, a devout woman considered to be one of God's most faithful servants.

During the visitation, Saint Michael advised Sister Antonia of his desire to be honored by a series of nine salutations. Each of these salutations were to correspond with the nine angelic choirs.

Christians practicing this devotion regularly in honor of Saint Michael are promised the presence of nine angels, one from each of the choirs, on their approach to the altar to receive the Sacrament. Their daily recital also assures us of the guidance of Saint Michael and all of the holy angels throughout our lives and beyond. This blessing is promised not only to the faithful Christians but also to their loved ones and relatives.

The chaplet begins by repeating the following invocation on the medal:-

O God, come to my assistance
O Lord, make haste to save me

Glory be to the Father, and to the Son, and to the Holy Spirit. As it was in the beginning, is now and ever shall be, world without end, Amen.

The nine salutations are recited as follows:-

First Salutation

At the intercession of Saint Michael and the heavenly choir of the Seraphim, may it please God to make us worthy to receive into our hearts the fire of His perfect charity. Amen.

One Our Father and Three Hail Marys in honor of the first angelic choir

Second Salutation

At the intercession of Saint Michael and the heavenly choir of the Cherubim, may God grant us the grace to abandon the ways of sin and follow the path of Christian perfection. Amen

One Our Father and Three Hail Marys in honor of the second angelic choir

Third Salutation

At the intercession of Saint Michael and the heavenly choir of the Thrones, may it please God to infuse into our hearts a true and earnest spirit of humility. Amen.

One Our Father and Three Hail Marys in honor of the third angelic choir

Fourth Salutation

At the intercession of Saint Michael and the heavenly choir of the Dominations, may it please God to grant us the grace to have dominion over our senses and to correct our depraved passions. Amen

One Our Father and Three Hail Marys in honor of the fourth angelic choir

Fifth Salutation

At the intercession of Saint Michael and the heavenly choir of the Powers, may God vouchsafe to keep our souls form the wiles and temptations of the devil. Amen.

One Our Father and Three Hail Marys in honor of the fifth angelic choir

Sixth Salutation

At the intercession of Saint Michael and the choir of the admirable celestial Virtues, may our Lord keep us from falling into temptations and deliver us from evil. Amen.

One Our Father and Three Hail Marys in honor of the sixth angelic choir

Seventh Salutation

At the intercession of Saint Michael and the heavenly choir of the Principalities, may it please God to fill our hearts with the spirit of true and hearty obedience. Amen.

One Our Father and Three Hail Marys in honor of the seventh angelic choir

Eighth Salutation

At the intercession of Saint Michael and the heavenly choir of Archangels, may it please God to grant us the gift of perseverance in the Faith and in all good works, that we may there be enabled to attain unto the glory of Paradise. Amen.

One Our Father and Three Hail Marys in honor of the eigth angelic choir

Ninth Salutation

At the intercession of Saint Michael and the heavenly choir of holy Angels, may God vouchsafe to grant that they may protect us during life, and after death may lead us into the everlasting glory of Heaven. Amen.

One Our Father and Three Hail Marys in honor of the ninth angelic choir

After the nine salutations, say 'Our Father' on each of the four remaining rosary beads; the first in honor of Saint Michael, the second in honor of St Gabriel, the third in honor of St Raphael and the fourth in honor of your personal Guardian Angel.

The devotion should be ended as follows:-

Saint Michael, glorious Prince, Chief and Champion of the Heavenly Host, guardian of the souls of men, conqueror of the rebel angels, steward of the palace of God under Jesus Christ, our worthy leader, endowed with superhuman excellence and virtue, free us from every ill, who with full confidence have recourse to thee; and by thine incomparable protection, enable us to make every day in the faithful service of our God. Amen.

Pray for us, most blessed Michael, Prince of the Church of Jesus Christ
That we may be made worthy of His promises

Finally pray-

Almighty and eternal God, who in thine own marvellous goodness and pity didst, for the common salvation of men, choose the glorious archangel Michael to be the Prince of thy church, make us worthy, we pray thee, to be delivered by his beneficent protection from all our enemies, that at the hour of our death, none of them may approach to harm us; rather grant that by the same archangel Michael we may be introduced in the presence of thy most high and divine majesty. Through the merits of the same Jesus Christ Our Lord. Amen.

Prayer to Saint Michael

Pope Leo XIII added this prayer in 1886 to the Leonine Prayers, which he had directed to be said after Low Mass two years earlier. The practice of reciting these prayers after Mass was suppressed in 1964. However, Pope John Paul II referred to the St Michael prayer in his Regina Coeli address of April 24, 1994, stating, "Although this prayer is no longer recited at the end of Mass, I ask everyone not to forget it and to recite it to obtain help in the battle against the forces of darkness and against the spirit of this world."

Sancte Michael Archangele,

defende nos in proelio;
contra nequitiam et insidias diaboli esto praesidium.
Imperet illi Deus, supplices deprecamur:
tuque, Princeps militiae Caelestis,
satanam aliosque spiritus malignos,
qui ad perditionem animarum pervagantur in mundo,
divina virtute in infernum detrude.
Amen.

Saint Michael the Archangel,

defend us in battle;
be our protection against the wickedness and snares of the devil.
May God rebuke him, we humbly pray:

and do thou, O Prince of the heavenly host,
by the power of God,
thrust into hell Satan and all the evil spirits
who prowl about the world seeking the ruin of souls.
Amen.

Prayer to Saint Michael II

In 1890, twenty years after the Capture of Rome had deprived the Pope of the last vestige of his temporal sovereignty, and the papal residence at the Quirinal Palace had been converted into that of the King of Italy, a much longer prayer to St. Michael, quite distinct from that in the Leonine Prayers, was approved for use:

O glorious Archangel St. Michael, Prince of the heavenly host, defend us in battle, and in the struggle which is ours against the principalities and Powers, against the rulers of this world of darkness, against spirits of evil in high places (Eph 6:12). Come to the aid of men, whom God created immortal, made in his own image and likeness, and redeemed at a great price from the tyranny of the devil (Wis 2:23-24, 1 Cor 6:20).

Fight this day the battle of the Lord, together with the holy angels, as already thou hast fought the leader of the proud angels, Lucifer, and his apostate host, who were powerless to resist thee, nor was there place for them any longer in Heaven. But that cruel, that ancient serpent, who is called the devil or Satan, who seduces the whole world, was cast into the abyss with all his angels (Rev 12:7-9).

Behold, this primeval enemy and slayer of man has taken courage, Transformed into an angel of light, he wanders about with all the multitude of wicked spirits, invading the earth in order to blot out the name of God and of his Christ, to seize upon, slay and cast into eternal perdition souls destined for the crown of eternal glory. This wicked dragon pours out, as a most impure flood, the venom of his malice on men of depraved mind and corrupt heart, the spirit of lying, of impiety, of blasphemy, and the pestilent breath of impurity, and of every vice and iniquity.

These most crafty enemies have filled and inebriated with gall and bitterness the Church, the spouse of the Immaculate Lamb, and have laid impious hands on her most sacred possessions (Lam 3:15).

In the Holy Place itself, where has been set up the See of the most holy Peter and the Chair of Truth for the light of the world, they have raised the throne of their abominable impiety, with the iniquitous design that when the Pastor has been struck, the sheep may be scattered.

Arise then, O invincible prince, bring help against the attacks of the lost spirits to the people of God, and bring them the victory.

The Church venerates thee as protector and patron; in thee holy Church glories as her defense against the malicious powers of this world and of hell; to thee has God entrusted the souls of men to be established in heavenly beatitude.

Oh, pray to the God of peace that He may put Satan under our feet, so far conquered that he may no longer be able to hold men in captivity and harm the Church. Offer our prayers in the sight of the Most High, so that they may quickly conciliate the mercies of the Lord; and beating down the dragon, the ancient serpent, who is the devil and Satan, do thou again make him captive in the abyss, that he may no longer seduce the nations.

Prayer to Saint Michael III

The 1890 prayer was replaced in 1902, a year and a half before the death of Pope Leo XIII, by a much shortened prayer:

O glorious Archangel St. Michael, Prince of the heavenly host, defend us in battle, and in the struggle which is ours against the principalities and Powers, against the rulers of this world of darkness, against spirits of evil in high places (Eph 6:12). Come to the aid of men, whom God created immortal, made in his own image and likeness, and redeemed at a great price from the tyranny of the devil (Wis 2:23-24, 1 Cor 6:20).

The Church venerates thee as protector and patron; to thee has God entrusted the souls of men to be established in heavenly beatitude.

Oh, pray to the God of peace that He may put Satan under our feet, so far conquered that he may no longer be able to hold men in captivity and harm the Church. Offer our prayers in the sight of the Most High, so that they may quickly conciliate the mercies of the Lord; and beating down the dragon, the ancient serpent, who is the devil and Satan, do thou again make him captive in the abyss, that he may no longer seduce the nations.

Novena

Saint Michael the Archangel,

loyal champion of God and His People.
I turn to you with confidence
and seek your powerful intercession.
For the love of God,
Who made you so glorious in grace and power,
and for the love of the Mother of Jesus, the Queen of the
Angels,
be pleased to hear our prayer.
You know the value of our souls in the eyes of God.
May no stain of evil ever disfigure its beauty.
Help us to conquer the evil spirit who tempts us.
We desire to imitate your loyalty to God and Holy Mother
and your great love for God and people.
And since you are God's messenger for the care of His people,
we entrust to you these special intentions:
...specific intentions are stated here....
Lord, hear and grant our special intentions for this Novena.
Amen.

Novena II

Glorious Saint Michael,

guardian and defender
of the Church of Jesus Christ,
come to the assistance of His followers,
against whom the powers of hell are unchained.
Guard with special care our Holy Father,
the Pope, and our bishops, priests,
all our religious and lay people,
and especially the children.
Saint Michael,
watch over us during life,
defend us against the assaults of the demon,
and assist us especially at the hour of death.
Help us achieve the happiness
of beholding God face to face
for all eternity. Amen.
Saint Michael,
intercede for me with God
in all my necessities,
especially.... "the intention is stated here"
Obtain for me a favorable outcome
in the matter I recommend to you.
Mighty prince of the heavenly host,
and victor over rebellious spirits,
remember me for I am weak and sinful
and so prone to pride and ambition.
Be for me, I pray,
my powerful aid in temptation and difficulty,

and above all do not forsake me
in my last struggle with the powers of evil.
Amen.

Litany to Saint Michael

Lord, have mercy on us.

Christ, have mercy on us.

Lord, have mercy on us. Christ, hear us.
Christ, graciously hear us.

God the Father of Heaven,
Have mercy on us.

God the Son, Redeemer of the world,
Have mercy on us.

God the Holy Spirit,
Have mercy on us.

Holy Trinity, One God,
Have mercy on us.

Holy Mary, Queen of the Angels, pray for us.
St. Michael the Archangel, pray for us.
Most glorious attendant of the Triune Divinity,
*Pray for us is repeated after each invocation
Standing at the right of the Altar of Incense,
Ambassador of Paradise,
Glorious Prince of the heavenly armies,
Leader of the angelic hosts,
Warrior who thrust Satan into Hell,
Defender against the wickedness and snares of the devil,

Standard-bearer of God's armies,
Defender of divine glory,
First defender of the Kingship of Christ,
Strength of God,
Invincible prince and warrior,
Angel of peace,
Guardian of the Christian Faith,
Guardian of the Legion of Saint Michael,
Champion of God's people,
Champion of the Legion of Saint Michael,
Guardian angel of the Eucharist,
Defender of the Church,
Defender of the Legion of Saint Michael,
Protector of the Sovereign Pontiff,
Protector of the Legion of Saint Michael,
Angel of Catholic Action,
Powerful intercessor of Christians,
Bravest defender of those who hope in God,
Guardian of our souls and bodies,
Healer of the sick,
Help of those in their agony,
Consoler of the souls in Purgatory,
God's messenger for the souls of the just,
Terror of the evil spirits,
Victorious in battle against evil,
Guardian and Patron of the Universal Church

Lamb of God, Who takes away the sins of the world,
Spare us, O Lord.

Lamb of God, Who takes away the sins of the world,
Graciously hear us, O Lord.

Lamb of God, Who takes away the sins of the world,
Have mercy on us.

Pray for us, O glorious Saint Michael,
That we may be made worthy of the promises of Christ.

Let Us Pray

Sanctify us, we beseech Thee, O Lord, with Thy holy blessing, and grant us, by the intercession of Saint Michael, that wisdom which teaches us to lay up treasures in Heaven by exchanging the goods of this world for those of eternity, Thou Who lives and reigns, world without end. Amen.

Relying, O Lord, upon the intercession of Thy blessed Archangel Michael, we humbly beg of Thee, that the Holy Eucharist in whose presence we kneel, may make our soul holy and pleasing to Thee. Through Christ Our Lord. R. Amen.

Help Against Enemies

Glorious Saint Michael, Prince of the heavenly hosts,

who stands always ready to give assistance to the people of
God;
who fought with the dragon, the old serpent,
and cast him out of heaven,
and now valiantly defends the Church of God
that the gates of hell may never prevail against her,
I earnestly entreat you to assist me also,
in the painful and dangerous conflict
which I sustain against the same formidible foe.
Be with me, O mighty Prince!
that I may courageously fight and vanquish that proud spirit,
whom you, by the Divine Power, gloriously overthrew,
and whom our powerful King, Jesus Christ,
has, in our nature, completely overcome;
so having triumphed over the enemy of my salvation,
I may with you and the holy angels,
 praise the clemency of God who,
having refused mercy to the rebellious angels after their fall,
has granted repentance and forgiveness to fallen man.
Amen.

Hymn to Archangel Michael

O angel! Bear, O Michael of great miracles, To the Lord my plaint.

Hearest thou? Ask of forgiving God Forgiveness of all my vast evil.

Delay not! Carry my fervent prayer To the King, the great King!

To my soul Bring help, bring comfort At the hour of its leaving earth.

Stoutly To meet my expectant soul Come with many thousand angels!

O Soldier! Against the crooked, wicked, militant world Come to my help in earnest!

Do not Disdain what I say! As long as I live do not desert me!

Thee I choose, That thou mayst save my soul, My mind, my sense, my body.

O thou of goodly counsels, Victorious, triumphant one, Angelic slayer of Antichrist!

Te Splendor

O Jesu, lifespring of the soul, The Father's power, and glory bright! Thee with the angels we extol; From Thee they draw their life and light.

Thy thousand thousand hosts are spread Embattled o'er the azure sky; But Michael bears Thy standard dread, And lifts the mighty cries on high.

He in that sign the rebel powers Did with their dragon prince expel; And hurl'd them from the heaven's high towers Down like a thunderbolt to hell.

Grant us with Michael still, O Lord, Against the Prince of Pride to fight; So may a crown be our reward, Before the Lamb's pure throne of light.

To God the Father glory be, And to his sole-begotten Son; The same, O Holy Ghost, to Thee, While everlasting ages run.

Ant. Most glorious Prince, Michael the Archangel, be thou mindful of us; here, and in all places, pray for us to the Son of God most high.

V. I wilt sing praises to Thee, my God, before the Angels.

R. I will adore Thee in Thy holy temple, and praise Thy Name. Let us pray.

O God, who in the dispensation of Thy providence dost admirably dispose the ministry of angels and of men; mercifully grant that the Holy Angels, who ever minister before Thy throne in heaven, may be the protectors also of our life on earth. Through Jesus Christ our Lord.

Made in United States
Orlando, FL
01 February 2025

58047526R00042